Fairy Spells

✳

Fairy Spells

✳

Seeing and Communicating
with the Fairies

✳

Claire Nahmad

✳

SOUVENIR
PRESS

This edition published in 2022

First published in Great Britain in 1997 by
Souvenir Press
an imprint of Profile Books Ltd
29 Cloth Fair
London
EC1A 7JQ
www.souvenirpress.co.uk

Copyright © Claire Nahmad 1997, 2022

Typeset by MRM Graphics

1 3 5 7 9 10 8 6 4 2

Printed and bound in Slovenia by DZS Grafik

The moral right of the author has been asserted.

A CIP catalogue record for this book is available from the British Library.

ISBN 978 1 80081 049 5

Fairy Spells

is dedicated, with love,

to Eva and Bernard Hanson

Contents

The Hours of the Angels

Whether you want to call on the fairies to reveal themselves, or to work one of the fairy spells in this book, you will need to learn the Hours of the Angels so that you can invoke the help of the ruling angel not only of that hour, but of the day you have chosen:

A.M.

12.00 – 1.00	Sachiel, Archangel of Jupiter (day: Thursday)
1.00 – 2.00	Anael, Archangel of Venus (day: Friday)
2.00 – 3.00	Auriel, Archangel of Uranus
3.00 – 4.00	Cassiel, Archangel of Saturn (day: Saturday)
4.00 – 5.00	Michael, Archangel of the Sun (day: Sunday)
5.00 – 6.00	Gabriel, Archangel of the Moon (day: Monday)
6.00 – 7.00	Samael, Archangel of Mars (day: Tuesday)
7.00 – 8.00	Raphael, Archangel of Mercury (day: Wednesday)
8.00 – 9.00	Sachiel, Archangel of Jupiter
9.00 – 10.00	Anael, Archangel of Venus
10.00 – 11.00	Auriel, Archangel of Uranus
11.00 – 12.00	Cassiel, Archangel of Saturn

P.M.

12.00 – 1.00	Michael, Archangel of the Sun (colours: gold and fire)
1.00 – 2.00	Gabriel, Archangel of the Moon (colours: silver and pale blue)
2.00 – 3.00	Samael, Archangel of Mars (colours: red and crimson)
3.00 – 4.00	Raphael, Archangel of Mercury (colour: yellow)
4.00 – 5.00	Sachiel, Archangel of Jupiter (colours: dark blue and violet)
5.00 – 6.00	Anael, Archangel of Venus (colours: green and turquoise)
6.00 – 7.00	Auriel, Archangel of Uranus (colours: all those of the spectrum)
7.00 – 8.00	Cassiel, Archangel of Saturn (colours: dark brown, grey and black)
8.00 – 9.00	Michael, Archangel of the Sun
9.00 – 10.00	Gabriel, Archangel of the Moon
10.00 – 11.00	Samael, Archangel of Mars

MIDNIGHT

11.00 – 12.00	Raphael, Archangel of Mercury

Introduction

I believe in fairies. These marvellous beings do exist, and I shall continue to remain insistent on that point. It is merely that we have lost the art of seeing and communicating with them.

There is at the present time, as there has been throughout two or more centuries of rationalistic thought, a body of opinion which insists that only the mundane sphere of knowledge relating to the physical world and its laws, and the report of these given by the five senses, is acceptable. Everything else is miscreant and to be reviled and shunned.

We can see how this particular form of fundamentalism has mechanised our world and robotised our response to it. Those who deplore such fundamentalism may be put in mind of Ahriman, a great demonic being who is Lord of Darkness in ancient Persian mythology, a spirit who wishes to imprison humanity in the darkness of matter so that we see life as the workings of a dead and soulless machine invested with an automatic impulse to sustain and procreate itself. As humankind conceives of the scheme of life as robotic in essence, so do we ourselves fall deeper and deeper into unconsciousness and become like robots. It is then that Ahriman attains his greatest power over our destiny.

Ahriman is the witherer, the destroyer, the Slayer of the Real. He works through the lower mind, which is the intellect. His arid breath consumes and shrivels vision, spirit, communion, inspiration. His is not the voice of reason, which steadies and secures, but the smooth, chilling voice of cynicism which drags us down and depresses us in the fathoms of matter so that our consciousness loses all sight and grasp of our true potential as inhabitants of a spiritual world of wonder and divine possibility.

It is the entombing of such divine possibility by the limitations of materialistic thinking that has blotted out our ability to see and communicate with the fairies, those ethereal nature spirits who, in a golden age long past, conjoined with humanity in brotherhood to create a paradise on earth. Since those times, the Ahrimanic impulse has taken over as human consciousness has moved ever deeper into the dark domain of matter, seeking to dominate, control and exploit the Earth.

As we begin to awaken to our lost spiritual heritage, denied us by materialist and rationalist inhibition, the visionaries of our age are able to see that our world is not the result of a blind and mechanical process whereby the phenomenon of humanity finds itself by sheer chance in an indifferent universe, but that the laws governing matter are such that the physical sphere can be stabilised and developed into a perfect receptacle for spirit. They assure us that gathering around our planet is an ethereal mantle of divine light composed of angelic substance, imbued with the vibrations of higher intelligence emanating from a pure and elevated source in the cosmos. If our planet and its suffering human cargo are to be healed and harmonised, we must rise in spirit, intent on creative endeavour, in order to earth this mystical power.

For this healing and harmonising of ourselves with our Mother Earth, we sorely need the help, not only of the angels and the great masters of the inner planes who are drawing near in order to guide and inspire us, but of the fairies who dwell within nature and who have a deep and intimate connection with our thoughts and feelings. Not only do the fairies build form in the vegetable kingdom in all its variety, they also build the essence of those subtle vehicles that are our mental and emotional bodies; for, just as we have a physical body miraculously composed of the elements of earth, so do we have finer bodies for our thought and feeling life composed of the etheric essence of those same four physical elements. The fairies help us to weave and sustain these bodies; indeed, they have secret access to them, so that they can lend inspiration to our mental and soul creations—our music, art, dance and literature are not created without their help, nor are our scientific and medical discoveries pioneered without their aid and blessing. Our human past and future—and our arid, apocalyptic present—are all inextricably bound up with the vital essence of the fairy world and its magical inhabitants.

It is vital at this time of particular environmental and spiritual crisis that we regain our lost ability to understand and communicate sympathetically with the fairies. The evolution of our souls (our true and deeper selves) and even our continued existence on this beautiful planet Earth may well depend on it. Seers and psychics assure us that in spite of our ravages of what the fairies hold most dear, in spite of the painful limitations of our truncated vision, the time is ripe and even urgent for the rediscovery of the enchanted fairy realms.

There is abroad and stalking us at the moment a peculiar form of emotional constriction that might be labelled 'spiritual embarrassment'. In the last century, sexual embarrassment abounded until Sigmund Freud and other thinkers began the task of dismantling it. How much more essential that spiritual embarrassment, concerned as it is with the deepest, the true source of life rather than just the outer manifestation of it via the sexual forces, mysterious as these are, should be overcome.

Despite this spiritual embarrassment, most of us will have retained from childhood a hidden knowledge pertaining to the wonder of the inner worlds of nature and the fairies, although we keep it secret from our adult, alienated selves. It is this sense of wonder and awe that we need to recapture before we can begin to approach the fairy realm; and the surest means of procuring it is to reclaim our childhood selves. Christ taught that we need to become as little children in order to enter the kingdom of heaven. The first mansion of this kingdom is the fairy world, where being unites in untold joy and blessing with the outer physical forms

on our Earth, thereby irradiating all nature with the essence of paradise. The spells and instructions in each chapter of this book are intended to nurture the childhood self, and to use them efficaciously it is necessary to become childlike, to trust, to love, to wonder—and to refuse to stay too serious for long! Then the fairies will approach, the spirit of childhood will enter us, and our burdens will fall away.

It has been given to the fairies to nurture the spirit of childhood throughout the universe. Watch young animals, young children, at play; their frolics and humour and delight in life are a direct gift of the fairies. Very young creatures readily receive these gifts because they have not yet been taught how to erect barriers that choke and stifle the life forces and so make the fairies withdraw. But it can be our mission to seek the renewal and rediscovery of that open, ageless and childlike self which the fairies will once again offer us. We were never intended to struggle alone, and it is the design of the universe that the fairies should bring us a sense of fun, of humour, and a zest for life. Without them life is grim indeed, full of toil and fatigue and needless sorrow. Yet with their inspiration we can at last begin to escape from, and indeed overcome, the tremendous gravity pull of earth, of matter itself. We have simply to keep the heart open, humble and childlike. Then we can put aside for ever the dreary—and literally deadly—cult of materialism with all its life-withering philosophy and usher in a new golden age for the blessing of Mother Earth and her ailing humanity.

1

The Enchanted Fairy Isle

---- ✳ ----

In order to develop fairy vision, the first step is to consider the power of the imagination. This is by no means to imply that fairies are imaginary and that what you will learn to see is mere whimsy. It is simply that we have forgotten the tremendous significance of the imagination, and the mystical reason why it was vouchsafed to us.

If we can think of our consciousness as comprising two spheres, one the lower mind and the other the higher, we can make a clear distinction between fantasy and imagination. Fantasy is about wish fulfilment; it concerns the lower mind and its egotistical indulgence of those yearnings and strivings to do with the personality and the everyday self. The artist Thetis Blacker tells us in her book *A Pilgrimage of Dreams* that she saw visions and underwent voyages of deep spiritual transformation in her dreaming life, and that she also experienced another type of vision, a mental vision in which she was repeatedly bowing on stage and graciously receiving the applause and bouquets of a huge audience in an opera house. The first type of vision belongs to the higher mind, the realm of the imagination; the second belongs to the lower mind, the dimension of fantasy.

The mystery schools teach that when sacred scriptures proclaim that humanity was made in the image of God, the real meaning of this divine truth is that we have been entrusted with the image-

creating power of God. We can partake of the marvellous inner reality of the cosmos and its worlds within worlds and seek knowledge of all things through this precious gift of the imagination.

Western society has very much relegated the imaginal faculties to a denigrated, back-seat position and exalted the status of the knowledge we receive through the intellect, so that only what is filtered through the channel of the intellect and the five senses is perceived as valid.

We have made a grave mistake in moving in this direction, because the intellect is a component of the lower mind which, until it begins to work in co-operation with the higher mind, remains dead to the true essence of life. It is the imagination that sparks into action the higher mental faculties, which are actually located in the heart—not the physical organ but the magical chakra, the vortex of energy at the centre of our being which connects us to spiritual reality. This mind-in-the-heart should be the zenith of our perception, with the intellect acting as handmaiden to channel, earth and balance the enlightenment—some call it 'pure reason'—that we receive from the heart-mind.

Because we have scoffed at the imagination for so long, our organs of spiritual perception have fallen into disuse and have gradually atrophied. Seers agree that the equipment with which we see fairies is a component of the physical eye, but it needs the stimulus of the spiritual organ behind the physical before this attribute can function. In order to revitalise our atrophied organs of spiritual perception, it is of benefit to read poetry (especially the nature poets), to listen to music by the masters of composition and by folk artists, and particularly to explore nature, to walk as far into the wilderness as possible, either alone or with a friend sympathetic to our purpose.

Here is an exercise to initiate this process. The ballad on page 18 is by an unknown Irish poet; its gentle rhythm and simple but vivid imagery will lead us faithfully into the fairy worlds, if we will but linger with the verses and take time to allow them to work their magic.

Let each image, each thought, slowly and beautifully take shape in your mind, like a bubble gradually forming on the bowl of a pipe when you gently blow down it. Resist the temptation to mentally gobble the images in the way that the intellect likes to, hastily sifting and collating so as to dominate the germ of thought in the words. It is this tendency of the intellect that we have to overcome. So refuse to allow it to drive you in such a way that, instead of savouring the immediacy of each living thought as it arises in the poem, you are rushing headlong to the next, fired by an obsession with speed and accumulation. This is what the intellect makes us do. To retrain it to become the handmaiden of the mind-in-the-heart we must insist on a pause after each image, each thought, so that the heart-mind may receive it from the intellect, then unite with the life already inherent in that image or thought. In this way we begin to see it clothed in its true radiance and mystery of form. Like our heartbeat, and the moment of silence and stillness that follows it, life in the spiritual worlds is composed of a rhythm of pulse and stillness; and the pulse of our intellect, followed by the stillness in which our intuition receives and transmutes into spiritual reality the substance it has been fed, represents the interplay of earthly and spiritual forces. This skilful warp and weft allows the true image to appear on the tapestry of our understanding, and it is the key that will open the door to the fairy worlds.

Commit specially to memory the fact that the Land of Faery has always been known to mortals as 'the Land of the Living Heart'. This in itself teaches us something of immense importance, because assuredly, until we bring life to our hearts, until the heart-mind is again vital, until we respond to life from our spiritual centre and cast off the dull obscurity of materialism, we shall never find Faery. The poet W. B. Yeats said that the country of the people of Faery was 'the heart of the world'. In turning away from the fairies, we lost access to the heart of the world, and to the fabulous breadth and depth of our human hearts. Here is the poem.

The Enchanted Fairy Isle

To Rathlin's Isle I chanced to sail
When summer breezes softly blew,
And there I heard so sweet a tale,
That oft I wished it could be true.
They said, at eve, when rude winds sleep,
And hushed is ev'ry turbid swell,
A mermaid rises from the deep,
And sweetly tunes her magic shell.

And while she plays, rock dell and cave
In dying falls the sound retain,
As if some choral spirits gave
Their aid to swell her witching strain.
Then summoned by that dulcet note,
Uprising to th'admiring view,
A fairy island seems to float
With tints of many a gorgeous hue.

And glittering fanes, and lofty towers,
All on this fairy isle are seen;
And waving trees, and shady bowers,
With more than mortal verdure green.
And as it moves, the western sky
Glows with a thousand varying rays;
And the calm sea, tinged with each dye,
Seems like a golden flood of blaze.

They also say, if earth or stone,
From verdant Erin's hallowed land,
Were on this magic island thrown,
For ever fixed, it then would stand;
But, when for this, some little boat
In silence ventures from the shore—
The mermaid sinks—hushed is the note,
The fairy isle is seen no more!

2

Fairy Days and Hours

※

Having begun gently to open the heart-centre with specially attuned musing and meditation on poetry, music and nature, it is time to actively seek out the fairies.

In preparation for this, it is wise to note that there are certain days, and hours of the day, which lend their aid to the mortal seeking Faeryland. These days and hours are impregnated with magical vibrations which thin the veil, woven by our inclination to cling to materiality, between our world and theirs. You will find it worth while to greet these fairy days and hours, if you are going to make practical use of them, with a ritual prayer to the deities concerned with fairy life. Among these are Pan, the Horned God, who is the masculine spiritual guardian of the fairies; and the three aspects of the Nature Goddess called Diana, Artemis and Aradia, who are concerned with the inspiration of the fairy people and, most interestingly, with our perception and knowledge of the fairy realm. These are the Greek names of these tutelary goddesses, who appear in Celtic mythology as the star goddess Ahrianrad, the moon goddess Bride or Bridget and the fairy goddess or queen Aine (pronounced 'Awnie'). It should be noted that some cults with unfortunate attitudes towards human sexuality, and towards the life forces of which that sexuality is an objectification, have adopted Pan as a god of darkness and lust. This creature has nothing to do with the true Pan, who is a gentle and joyous god.

Light a candle to intone your prayer. Word it as you choose, only taking care to be respectful and to formulate your request to develop fairy vision very clearly in your heart, your mind and your words. Your candle should be white, green, blue, orange or brown. (Simple white is perhaps best of all.)

Having communed with the fairy deities, ask for the care and protection of your own guardian angel. The fairies can be mischievous! But it is important to understand that, although they are likely to play pranks at first and lead you something of a merry dance as you attempt to discover them, you must never allow exasperation or distress to overtake you. The fairies are an old and wise people—'O so old! / Thousands of years, if all were told,' the poet Yeats proclaims. They will test you, perhaps severely, for good humour and goodwill. They will never reveal themselves, befriend or grant favours to ill-willed, bad-tempered or petty-natured humans, so if you have had a bad day, postpone your fairy-hunting until you feel better! You must take all of their tricks in good part, or you will be unable to develop fairy vision.

As well as the list of dates that follows, the days and vigils (eves) of the saints are propitious for communicating with the fairies, especially the night of 5 January, the Feast of St Ceera.

FAIRY DAYS

The calends of each month (the first day) are especially favoured:

| Imbolc (1 February) | Beltane (1 May) |
| Lammas (1 August) | Samhain (1 November) |

Other good days to seek out the fairies are:

Lady Day (25 March)   Walpurgis Night (May Day Eve)
Midsummer   Eve   Midsummer   Day   Hallowe'en
Christmas Eve   Christmas Day   The first days of spring, summer, autumn and winter (21 March, 21 June,

21 September and 21 December, respectively)   New
Year's Eve   New Year's Day   Whit Sunday

The great holy days or festivals of all the religions attune those
who observe them to rarefied vibrations throughout their duration,
so that the start of Ramadan, the Buddhist New Year, the North
Indian Sarasvati Puja (a spring festival in honour of the goddess
of learning, wisdom and the arts), Mardi Gras, the April Flower
Festival in Japan—all these are good days to go in search of the
fairies.

Monday, Tuesday, Thursday, Friday and Sunday have all been
cited as good days of the week to see fairies, although I have never
found anything amiss with Woden's Day or Saturn's Day either!

Fairy Hours

The most auspicious times for seeing the fairies are the early hours
of the morning as dawn breaks, the noon hour, as evening falls
(and especially that hour in spring and summer just before the
shadows begin to lengthen) and midnight. The fleeting moments
of sunrise and sunset are times of particular fairy enchantment,
when the songs of birds sweeten and all the world seems to fall
under spell.

The most favourable conditions for seeing fairies are sunshine,
the muted light of evening or dawn, or the bright white light of
a full moon—although any moonlit night is believed to vouchsafe
visions of the fairy host. New moon, and the last night of the old
moon—bidding farewell to the enchanted western isles, as legend
says—are nights of fairy magic too, when the folk of Elfame can
be seen at their revels.

3

Fairy Tricksters

———— ✳ ————

When we knock on the portals of Faeryland, they are unlikely to swing open immediately. We will be tried and tested, not only for our good nature and good humour (see Chapter Two) but also for our purity of purpose. If we wish truly to love the fairy folk, to learn from them and to embrace their wisdom, to be guided by them in our everyday behaviour as we relate to nature, to be filled with the divine light with which they work and to be touched profoundly by the fairy joy, then eventually they will grant us communion and fairy vision. But if our intention in seeking them out is rooted in idle curiosity or ignorant spying and voyeurism, we may expect to be pixie-led—and we will probably be pixie-led anyway, at the beginning of our venture, just so that they can ensure that our apparently best intentions are not bogus!

There are several methods that the fairies might employ to put us to the test. Two of which I have had personal experience involved the water fairies, or undines.

Once when I was a child I decided to clear a little pond enclosed by meadows which was filled with debris from nearby houses. At first the fairies were very hostile. Their environment had been despoiled and poisoned by human thoughtlessness. There was a strange, uneasy atmosphere around the pond; the waters swirled menacingly over what seemed to be black, sullen, bottomless depths as, with the help of a friend, I dragged out the stinking rubbish. We carried out this operation from the edges, but no matter how careful I tried to be, I was always pushed into the stagnant waters several times as I dredged. I make a distinction between slipping and being pushed in—there is a difference between losing one's footing and being hurled, somewhat astonished, into the water! I was aware of the 'pond dwellers' and the fairies living in the trees and reeds growing on the pond's edges, and I knew that it was these magical hidden folk who were responsible for my regular dips. As the weeks went by, the pushing in became less malevolent and much more playful. In time, the little pond became a place of repose and beauty, a meeting-place between the worlds where one could step into a radiant dimension of deep enchantment—a dimension of magical peace which thrilled with dynamic energies of wonder and revelation. My heart-mind learned much there. And in the end there was no more precipitation into the water!

My second experience concerns fairy restriction rather than fairy resentment.

With a companion, I had begun to visit the shores of a wild and remote lake. We went both during the day and at night, and saw many mysterious things, usually at twilight or as the first stars appeared. I became enthralled with this world of wonders and one night I decided to visit the secret lake alone.

I set out, accompanied by my little dog. As we approached the lake, before reaching the shore, I began to feel very oppressed and breathless, not from exertion but because there seemed not to be enough oxygen in the air. My dog stood still and refused to take another step forward. At the same time, my feeling of oppression began to change into extreme apprehension, tantamount to fear. Within a few seconds I seemed to receive a clear message—just a mental impression—that I must not try to get nearer to the lake, or penetrate the woods in either direction: it was imperative that I turn towards home immediately.

I obeyed this command rather sadly, because I had wanted to draw close to the fairies and spirits abroad in the woods and the

lake, and felt that I was being banished to the world of humdrum human concerns and trivial occupations. Yet, in retrospect, I am inclined to wonder whether it was not more of a friendly warning, issued simply for the sake of my own safety. Although the fairies are joyful and childlike, and make sport of their duties and are never tyrannised by them, they do have intensely magical rituals to perform which are the language of the innermost mysteries of the Earth; and it may not be safe or wise for us mortals, with our frail and limited psyches, set around with a thorn-hedge of preconditioning, to be present when they work their sublimest magic. All the same, I am certain that the fairies *do* bar the way to humans at times when it would in fact be safe to join them in their revels, simply because they do not want us there! If you encounter this barring of the way—and although nothing visible happens it is unmistakable—it helps to ask out loud for the obstacle to be dissolved. You might say something along these lines:

> *I come with respect and peace in my heart for the people of Elfame, and I will not try to venture where you forbid me to enter. I do not wish to trespass or to disturb you, but I would dearly love to come amongst you and be your companion for a while. If you can do me this honour, please give me a sign. May the eternal love and the deep peace of the Great Spirit be always with the people of Elfame.*

Send out a blessing from your heart-centre in the shape of a golden star, six-pointed and undivided (unlike the Star of David), and shower its gentle light over the fairies. Then wait. Listen to your heart's core. The block may lift, so that you will be able to go forward. But never, never proceed if you feel that it is still in place, because to do so would be dangerous. Resolve to be patient, and go home without allowing yourself to feel disappointed, ready to try again another night, as many times as it takes, to be allowed into Faeryland. If you try to disregard the wishes of the fairies, you will come to grief. They are not to be trifled with, and you must have sincere and heartfelt love and respect for them, and in all your dealings with them—otherwise, it is unsafe to approach them or their haunts.

This barring of the way is quite different from the Fairy Terror, which has been experienced by many people during daylight hours when wandering alone on moors or through woods. Wherever there is lonely wilderness, away from the dwellings of men, the fairies make their haunts; and it is here that they will put the Fairy Terror on anyone who, wittingly or unwittingly, draws too near the scene of their revels. If you can overcome the Fairy Terror, then it is likely that you will be rewarded with the fairies' friendship; but conquering the Terror is no easy task. Those who have been the victim of it say that it is overwhelming and dispensed with a deadly swiftness, so there is no time to resort to rational thought in an attempt to resolve the situation. Nevertheless, there is a little spell that protects from it, if the victim can find the presence of mind to put it into operation.

A Spell to Give Protection from the Fairies

If the Fairy Terror should fall on you, or if you fear hurt or malice from the fairies, without delay picture yourself as stepping into the disc of a huge golden sun which has six golden rays blazing from its heart, giving it the shape of a star. Feel yourself safe and protected at the centre of this star, and then let it become a perfect golden disc containing a golden equal-sided cross. The centre of this cross is where you are. Feel your heart, and the heart of this cross-of-light-within-the-circle-of-light, as one; from your heart will grow a perfect rose, red-pink in hue, as fragrant as the musk of paradise. Gently breathe out this sweet fragrance of the rose to the fairies and the malice they are sending after you, for this perfume is pure love. Then say aloud:

I send unconditional love and the sweet blessing of the Heavenly Rose to the fairies, and to those spirits who would do me harm. Peace to all beings. May the grace of the Great Spirit be upon your groves, your courts, your revels and your Country-under-Ground.

When you have said these words, be aware of the cross and the rose still, but now picture yourself in a violet cloak, of a radiant substance that makes it glow like a bright violet jewel. This cloak must form the shape of an egg around you, from above your head to beneath your feet. Wherever you go while you stay within reach of the fairies, you must wear it, this violet egg encasing you. Next, call upon the protection of the good angels, and ask your own guardian angel to enfold you in her unfailing protection. Then say aloud:

I who walk with angels, would walk with the fairies.

Wait a while, and if no sign is given, repeat the words. If, after you have spoken them a third time, there is no sign or any opening of the way, retrace your steps, content in the knowledge that the fairies have heard you and will give heed to your request if they find you worthy.

It is important to understand that practice is required before this spell can be worked effectively. Your focus must be on your heart-centre throughout—always work from the heart, not from the head. The same advice applies to the forming of the imagery: do not work hard at the mental level—instead, just allow the images to form beautifully and easily, without effort, in the peaceful gaze of your imagination. Learn the steps and stages of the spell 'by heart' (an apt phrase!) before seeking the fairies; and remember—even if it is necessary, initially, to protect yourself from their resentment—always to be relaxed and ready for humour when you seek them out. Be gentle, be humorous, be humble; and eventually the good people of Elfame will welcome you.

As well as the Fairy Terror, which is a blind panic that descends like a bolt from the blue and has no rational object, there are a number of other fairy pranks you may be subjected to. In no case should you ever panic or express resentment, but use the fairy protection spell and be ready to laugh off your confusion or discomfiture.

The fairies are able to create the illusion of altering the landscape so that, even though you may be familiar with the terrain, it is quite possible to become hopelessly lost. People speak of wandering round and round, perhaps in a field, looking for an opening which they know is there but which has mysteriously disappeared! There are frequent instances of this particular fairy trickery, so if you are the subject of it, avoid exhausting yourself by wandering about, find somewhere to sit down, and perform the fairy protection spell that I have just described. The illusion will fade before long. There is an old country spell to break the fairies' charm which bids you take off your coat and put it on the wrong way round (if not a coat, then any item of clothing you are wearing before the illusion takes hold). But I admit that I have heard of several instances where this spell was entirely ineffective.

The Fairy Wind is another phenomenon the Good Folk use to scare off intruders. This can manifest as a great rushing, roaring storm wind that springs up suddenly during calm weather; or it can appear as a strange gust that causes something extraordinary to happen, such as displacing a certain object while others nearby remain undisturbed—or even sometimes displacing a person! Incidents abound in folklore of mortals reportedly being spirited away by the fairies to distant lands, returning after a few hours utterly exhausted and suffering from a disorientation very similar to jetlag. The folktales insist that such journeys involve bodily transportation, and certain psychic experiments suggest that physical objects can indeed be mysteriously conducted through space (the modern term is 'teleportation').

It is unlikely, though, that the fairies will resort to such alarming tactics when they are sincerely sought after with proper humility and goodwill. It is much more probable that they will use the agency of the Fairy Wind to speak to our heart-mind. It is important to recognise that there is meaning, there are messages, in the murmurs and swells and quietenings of the Fairy Wind.

While I was on the shores of my own secret lake, the Fairy Wind would arise—often towards evening, in the early twilight— and speak with the voice of some ineffable, all-pervading spiritual being. Its sighs and whispers, its sudden lilting dance across the waters, its hushing lulls and gradual passionate rising were a mantra to set free the human soul. Like a lover, the voice of the wind spoke to my deepest, innermost faculties of hearing and understanding, and drew away the veil between circumscribed mortal perception and the Land of the Living Heart.

This moment is a revelation of ecstasy; and the heart-mind perceives not only the wonder of the fairy realms, but the true essence of humankind and the fact that every human being has been entrusted with a treasure beyond imagining, to be invested in his or her own development. It becomes clear that the noblest denizens of the most exquisite of the fairy realms are profoundly linked with our own evolution and spiritual destiny; and although it is hard to withdraw from this magical vista, something of the vision persists when one touches down on present-day planet Earth again, to cheer and inspire, to renew the living waters of the spirit, and to nurture the unfolding dream towards a manifest reality.

This enchanted Fairy Wind, with its songs and stories, its secrets and dreams, its poetry and dancing—because the fairies are forever trying to persuade us to dance, as well as to smile!—is surely the wind's very soul. And once one has been courted by and has given ear to the Fairy Wind, one cannot hear the keening and sighing of the winds of our human world without hearing anew the soul of the wind and its magical abundance of secret stories.

If you are buffeted with unfriendly intent by this Fairy Wind, do not be alarmed. Open your soul and begin to listen. The Fairy Wind will have a message for you, even if it is a hostile one. Don't be afraid. Whisper back upon the wind: 'I come with respect and peace in my heart for the people of Elfame . . .' (see page 27). Before long the Fairy Wind will begin to murmur soothingly, and in its dying and rising you will hear the language of the fairy world. If there is a well defined message, such as branches of trees blasting across your path, or an article of clothing blowing off so that you have to retrace your steps to retrieve it, do not try to make progress until you have whispered your message of peace and good intent—and then not until an opening of the way is granted (you will sense this).

Another well known trick of the fairies is to assault unfortunates

with the Fairy Grass (or 'hungry grass'). Wandering through the countryside, a poor mortal steps on turf magically impregnated by mischievous fairies with a waiting elemental. The human chakras, or gateways permitting entry of spiritual and astral energies, open up, and the elemental takes temporary possession, giving rise to a hunger in the human being that feels like a kind of insanity and is only relieved by desperate gorging. After the feast, the elemental leaves, and there is no further problem—except that there have been cases where it has remained, causing the constant urge to overeat and commit other excesses. Dermot Mac Manus, author of the excellent book on fairies called *The Middle Kingdom*, states that this phenomenon is confined to Ireland; but in fact I have come across several reported cases in England. One in particular, concerning an English wisewoman who claimed to be able to cure conditions where the elemental continued to possess the etheric body of the victim, was extraordinary indeed. Her trick was to prepare a meal imbued with strong savoury aromas and to waft it about under the nose of her patient, who was under special orders to restrain the agonising gluttony that had taken over his or her life. Not being gratified at once, as had hitherto always been the case, the elemental actually rose up into the mouth of its host to demand satisfaction. It was then sucked into a bottle with the help of spells and wise-craft. Not only did the wisewoman effect cures this way, but she also dried and preserved the bodies of the elementals, which had assumed some sort of physical form within the incarcerating confines of the bottle; and she made a practice of hanging these 'efts', as she called them, over her hearth on the chimney-breast for all to see!

When seeking communication with the fairies, it is wise to remember that humankind and the citizens of the elemental worlds are at war. This is a war that *we* have initiated by our wholesale rape and pillage of Mother Earth. As soon as they understand that we want to offer the hand of brotherhood and actively express respect and love for them and the world of nature which is their domain, the fairies will lay down their arms.

4

Fairy Spells

———— ✳ ————

This little collection of spells is offered for the development of your fairy vision. If performed faithfully and with sincerity, they will certainly bring results, although these may at first be very subtle. Trust that your workings will be fruitful; and gradually, unmistakable evidence will gently unfold, proving their effectiveness.

An ancient spell for seeing the fairies comes to us down the centuries from our magical past, that Celtic twilight which confounds the mundane perceptions of our present materialist culture; but its association of herbs with fairy magic has its roots in a time that was remote even to the Celts, and that informed and inspired their spiritual vision in all its intensity.

Fairy Oil
(From the manuscripts of Sarah Greaves)

There is an old spell which gives directions for making a Fairy Oil that will enable one to look into the magical fairy worlds. This oil is to be made up in spring and left to settle so that it can be put to use on the Fairy Days.

Sweet herbs and summer flowers have many potencies, and it is good to use these; but they cannot do all the work for you; you must prepare your own soul so that you may see fairies; and this means loving them and their world of nature, loving the Great Heart which holds us all, and seeking them in their haunts at the right time and in the right way. Thus, offering humility and listening to inner guidance, may you see the fairies, and if you prepare the oil, prepare it with a charm of your own at the hours of Sachiel (see page 8), and let your charm be a prayer to the God of meadows and forests, and the Great God and Goddess of All, that you may enter the fairy realm without harm, that the fairies may come to know and love you, and that you may know and love them.

Here is the wortcunning to be followed in preparing the Fairy Oil: put a tankard of corn oil into a green glass jar, and bless it with charms. Gather eglantine, the leaves of the briar, the buds of the hollyhock, the flowers of wild thyme (the young ripening tops of the fragrant wild grass), the shooting buds of young hazel, yarrow flowers, meadow-sweet and rue, and the sweet grass from inside a fairy-ring [the circular stretches of deeper, lush green grass whose material origin is the action of a fungus, but which have a connection with the ethereal life of the fairies]. Pluck some marigold flowers from the garden. If you do not have any, the humble but lovely field-marigold will suffice [commonly called the dandelion]. Gather your herbs and flowers from those that grow towards the east; and at Cassiel's hour (see page 8), steep your posy in the corn oil, again summoning blessings with runes.

Leave it to ripen in the sun (the jar must be covered or stoppered) for three days; then you may pour out the oil into smaller glass jars, as small as may be. Into each one put seven drops of rose-oil, with seven supplications to the Earth Angel to help you to see the fairy folk, and stopper well. A light touch of the oil is to be put on to your eyelids, upon your brow, into the hollow of the throat, on to each finger tip and rubbed into the wrists before proceeding into the wild. It would be well to do this at Cassiel's hour or Sachiel's hour, if you conveniently may; and then you must venture out alone to see the fairies, even if that be only into your own garden under the early moon, or just at sunrise, noon, or as the evening dew falls.

If you can wash your eyes in the pure dew, which some say is the sweat of the stars, that is good; and mark well the Fairy Days, though others may be tried, for the fairies are always with us.

If you find the instruction to prepare the fairy oil 'with a charm of your own' puzzling, use the following invocation to call fairies into the garden. Choose one of the fairy days and times to use it, and call upon the angel of the hour—Gabriel seems to be particularly sympathetic towards these workings—if his/her hour is convenient (see page 8).

> Fairy host, from the wild
> Come and tend this plot awhile;
> Come dancing from the hollow hill
> To raise the power and do God's will;
> Make your revels in my garden,
> May this soil be fairy-trodden!
> Each herb and flower, each garden tree
> Set each lovely spirit free!
> May all be hung with globes of light
> From deepest Elfame, fair and bright.
> Fairies, heed this pledge I tell
> To honour you and treat you well!

The Northern Lights Fairy Spell

When the firmanent is lighted up with meteoric phenomena, and the Merry Dancers assume their pretty gowns of many colours and make great sport up and down the curtain of the night sky until they are in a fair frolic and frenzy, these Northern Lights are come to let you know that the evening is full of fire and magic, and the season ripe for spells and craftworking.

Therefore, coax a cat (better if she be black) onto your lap, and sit alone with her in the garden, stroking her until a sheen appears on her coat, and she purrs contentedly. Have at your elbow a nipperkin of wine in a small vessel, and at the cat's first stretch, anoint her lightly with the wine, making the holy sign of the cross upon her head, and then do the same for yourself.

Gently grasp the end of her tail and stroke it three times swiftly over your left eye, and then over your right, saying:

> Elves of the night, enchant my sight,
> Your forms for to see in moon or sunlight;

With this spell and with this sign
I pri'thee, forward my design.

Let Puss run off, and steal away to your bedchamber, there to contemplate the moon and the stars and all the magical lights of the sky from your lattice. If you have found favour with the fairies, then mystic dreams will come to you that night, and afterwards you will begin to see the Little People at their revels, faintly at first, but yet more clear, more lucid, as the fairy-enchantment blesses ever deeper your inner seeing.

The Spell of the Fairy Thimbles

If a young maid will look for the first harebells of spring, which are called 'fairy thimbles' and are witch's flowers, and then count them up three times as the sun is rising or the dew is falling, she can summon the fairies. She, on leaving, must address them thus:

'Fairies, I have sought your bower;
I now retire, and bless your power.'

She must curtsey three times to the fairies, and the magic of the glade will go with her.

The Oakleaf Fairy Spell

If a maid that is deep in love will go with her suitor to a lonely place in the meadows or the woods, or to the moors, and place within her own and her lover's shoe a single oakleaf; and if they both will wait there and contemplate their love, and speak it to one another as evening falls and the stars come out, they will, if their patience is good, behold the fairy host as they come to gambol and sport in the wilds.

The Four-leaf Clover Fairy Spell

If a maid will slip a four-leaf clover into her left shoe, and tie a garland of myrtle and clover around her brow, she will see the fairies as the moon comes up.

The Toadstone Fairy Spell

On Midsummer's Eve or Midsummer's Night, or upon any beautiful night of the year, especially when the moon is full, you may offer a gift to the fairies. This, if it is done with a sincere heart, is a sure way to win their confidence and favour.

Bake a little oaten cake, or put honey and wine into a pot, or, better still, offer the fairies a song, or a dance, or a verse that you have made up, or that you find pleasing. Say aloud before you begin the work: 'This is for the fairies'; and say it again when the gift is given, which should be done out of doors, in a sequestered place, wild and lonely.

Then, very soon, most likely the next day, you will find that the fairies give something back to you; keep your eyes sharp for their gift, but let not your giving be done because you think that such a gift will be given in return, neither expect anything; keep a look-out for it, all the same. It is certain that very soon you will find some curious but lovely object from nature, or you may find some silver money. Whatever you find, keep it forever, because that is a sacred gift, and will bring you good luck and happiness.

Most often the item you find will be a toadstone—a round pebble with mysterious and beautiful mottlings and marks, seeming to glow with many delicate hues. Keep this by you, and sleep with it under your pillow; according to wiselore, these stones are the mystic jewel that is to be found in the head of the toad. She (or he) who holds such a stone will be lucky in love, wise in divination, and blessed in life.

5

Fairy Haunts

---- ✳ ----

When we go in search of the fairy haunts, the power of intuition must come into play. It can generally be said that fairies inhabit wild and lonely places; yet they can also be found in town parks, and in our gardens. These are the smaller fairies, the flower fairies so faithfully depicted by Cicely Mary Barker, Margaret Tarrant and other painters. They are delightful beings, and all that has been said about the necessary attitude to fairies applies to them. But they are not the noble fairies, who appropriate human stature and who are custodians of human culture: these fairies are a deeply artistic and creative people, and the realms of song and storytelling, music and dance, poetry, drama and art belong to them. They know the deepest secrets of the earth, of nature and matter, and they are masters of all crafts—in Ireland, for instance, particular facility in the art of needlework is heralded as the special gift of the fairies.

These fairies inhabit fairy forts or raths, which are hills or mounds, natural or man-made, deep in the wilds. Within these hills are the fairy courts and palaces, where the people of Elfame move without restriction, as if in space, for it is only to us that matter seems dense and impenetrable. They also hold court in open places, in forests and woods and by the shores of sequestered lakes and pools.

Certain trees and flowers hold special vibrations for them, and where these grow in wild abundance the fairies are sure to congregate. The whitethorn, also known as the hawthorn or may tree, is perhaps the best-loved tree of the fairies, although as the old country saying 'Fairy folks are in old oaks' suggests, oak trees are also especially favoured. Lone trees are often fairy trees. If a tree is gnarled and mysterious in form, or generates a strongly magical personality it is almost certain to be a fairy tree. Joan of Arc, in the transcripts of her trial, was accused of 'dancing round the fairy tree'. This 'fairy tree' was just such a blessed and healing tree, where gifts were left to the fairies and to the Goddess for the granting of miracles. All trees have spirits and a consciousness of their own; but the fairy tree always has lush foliage and emits a venerable, healing aura—although sometimes it can seem hostile and jealously reclusive, because of the fairies' resentment of human intrusion. To recognise such trees is a matter of intuition. The lone fairy thorn is especially recognisable, as these often assume fantastical shapes and configurations.

Fairy trees are especially honoured because the fairies dance around them at certain times of the year, and hold their revels beneath and among their boughs. Potent and particular energies are produced by this activity, which makes fairy trees blessed beings.

If you come across a fairy tree, stand and meditate beside it for a while if you can, because this will help you to develop fairy vision. Do not try to probe the tree's mysteries; rather, seek to open your heart to receive them in humility. See the life of the tree rising from its roots and travelling along every branch and into every twig and leaf and bud like a white flame, the breath of the Great Spirit which the fairies joyfully celebrate. Enter into this fairy joy, and you will draw near to the nature spirits.

As well as the important fairy thorn, and the magical and majestic oak, other fairy trees and shrubs are the rowan, bramble, ash, blackthorn, elder, birch, apple, hazel, aspen, bay, lilac, willows (including the osier), alder, holly, broom, pine, beech and Scots pine. Any tree, of course, has the potential to become a fairy tree, but these seem to be the particular favourites.

Fairies love flowers and tend them, presiding over the life-cycle of the plants, replenishing them with their energies and suffusing them with their own vivid and happy hues. When we look at the gown of summer lying over the land, we are contemplating fairy colours, and the colours of the robes of the angels who dispense their own spiritual force to the fairies.

When searching out fairy haunts, remember that any meadow or stretch of ground resplendent with masses of wild flowers indicates a fairy presence. Two of the flowers which the fairies especially love are the golden ragwort, said to be used by them to facilitate flying energy when they travel over long distances, and the briar rose, a plant that has a highly evolved soul.

Look for unusual features in a wild landscape, because those which suggest idiosyncrasy and mystery, which breathe their own atmosphere within the surrounding countryside and which bear a certain rugged eccentricity that speaks of otherworldliness are likely to be fairy forts. Look also for the brilliant pieces of black stone, like jet, that are the fairies' gifts to mortals and will bring us an ever-deepening understanding of the nature folk. I have come upon wild meadows bright with many-coloured grasses and mosses glowing like jewels, or tufted with strange little hillocks and mounds covered with shining white pebbles. A surprising number of these miniature Edens still exist, even quite close to human dwellings and in spite of the encroachment of the land brought about by prairie farming methods. Before you begin your exploration of the countryside, ask to be guided to the fairy haunts, and if you persist and show that your intention is serious you will eventually be led to the sites of their strange and beautiful forts.

If, at all times when seeking the fairies, you keep the heart-mind open and receptive, you will be able to 'test the waters' to find out whether a certain place is blessed with the fairy presence.

6

Fairies and Angels

✳

As Christianity began to outpace the Old Religion and its philosophy, fairies came gradually to be perceived as intermediate beings not wicked enough to belong to the demonic legions—although the Church often insisted that they did—yet not good enough to dwell with the angelic hierarchy in heaven. There is a strange and twisted half-truth in this belief.

Fairies certainly are deeply devoted and connected to our Mother Earth. Though possessed of individual being and intelligence, they are nevertheless at the same time manifestations of her spirit, as in fact we ourselves are, although we are busy truncating and impeding our consciousness rather than expanding it. Fairies are essentially linked with the angels; they are their faithful handservants at the earthly level—in fact, we might call them the last link in the chain of command.

There are angels of light and angels of darkness, and the fairies definitely serve the former. There *are* gruesome creatures who serve the dark angels, but we need have no fear of them. If we are unfortunate enough to encounter them, we can simply step into the heart of the (undivided) six-pointed star, and wrap around ourselves a shining white cloak of protection, simultaneously calling on our own guardian angel to protect us (which it cannot do unless we ask). The Creatures of the Shadow will then be disempowered, unable to do us any harm. There are also great spirits of nature whom it is not safe for us to approach or look upon. Sometimes these spirits are simply too majestic in their potency and vitality for our weaker life force to withstand. Occasionally, they are angry and hostile because of our self-initiated alienation from the beloved, sacred Earth which they hold so dear; seeing that we behave as if we held her in contempt, they scorn us accordingly. Yet we could only ever encroach upon these noble beings by overriding each and every inner warning and restraining voice that arises from our intuition and heart-mind; and even then, our angelic companions, and our human spiritual guides, are ever on the alert to protect us from such mishaps. It was from these awesome beings, I half suspect, that I was protected when my way was barred on the night of my excursion to the shores of the secret lake.

There are four mighty archangels which represent the four elements from which the physical universe is composed. These archangels are the consciousness, the sustaining structure of every atom, of matter itself. They are the breadth and depth of the great lessons of the soul which every human being must learn, symbolised by the north, south, east and west points upon the medicine wheel; traditionally, the south is the place of Fire, the north of Earth, the west of Water and the east of Air.

Although the fairies each correspond to one or another of the archangels, so that there are sylphs of the air, undines of the water, salamanders of fire and gnomes of earth, all of them are gathered together in the exquisite robes of the great Earth Angel, whose sweetness and serene majesty are linked to the Great Goddess, the mother aspect of the Godhead, she who commands and breathes forth all the angelic and elemental life of the universe. And, through this mystical connection, the Earth Angel is also associated with the goddesses of the Earth and the moon and the planet Venus, who dispense the abundance and fecundity of the Great Goddess, and her mother-love in all its healing, wisdom and beauty.

The vast angelic host working under the direction of the Earth Angel preside over the joy-filled fairy folk as they eternally dance through her robes, which permeate the living world and are of the essence of life itself, its pulse and rhythms expressing themselves as music and colour on the etheric planes.

Strands of light connect the simplest and tiniest of the fairy workers to their fairy brethren a little higher up in the hierarchy. It has been posited that these miniature fairies, who swarm among the flowers and busily attend to the minutiae of their needs, and who do not gradually evolve into more advanced beings as the higher fairies do but simply die away like an autumn leaf when their spring and summer work is done, have an awareness somewhat akin to that of insects. This is not my view, because although these little beings are not individualised in any profound sense and are really just angelic thought-forms—as are the flowers they tend—they are quite different from material-bodied beings, which vibrate at a much lower frequency. Also, these fairies are invested with the divine human structure, perfect in its etheric pattern, which makes all the fairies such a delight to behold. Moreover, they partake of the fairy joy, so it is evident that even the humblest of the fairy workers share in a spiritual consciousness.

The more individualised fairies with which these exquisite little troops of miniature beings are linked by threads of light are the elves, gnomes and undines who still inhabit our gardens and parks when they sense a concord of the spirit with their human brethren, but who have mainly fled into the wild heart of the countryside. Their connective threads lengthen so that they can still direct and inspire the little fairy workers. These fairies, in turn, are attached by this linkage of shining strands to the nobler fairy beings, who exercise a wider influence in the scheme of nature. As the scintillating threads reach each higher sphere, they gather together into something like a lover's knot, then rise again to the next level. Here, in the order described, the angels themselves begin at last to appear, lovingly and joyfully guiding and directing the fairies as if by sounding notes upon the silver threads like the vibrating strings of a piano. If you hum the diatonic scale—the eight notes of an octave sung as do-re-mi-fa-so-la-ti-do—you will grasp the

structure of these planes as they ascend. When the Earth Angel and the co-workers under her direction have completed an octave, another begins, reaching into heavenly dimensions and realms beyond our comprehension.

The joy and the wonder of all this is that we too are corded into life in just the same way. By special dispensation from the Great Spirit of all, we are linked with each dimension, every sphere of life both physical and spiritual; and it is our sacred and ecstatic duty to learn to recognise and treasure these bonds in full consciousness and knowledge of their sanctity. Perhaps the best way of doing this is to throw open wide our hearts and minds to the angels and fairies who vitalise the physical universe and who are the mystical forces we feel and respond to in the nature kingdom.

The fairies commune with their higher brethren and with the angels through the agency of prayer, ritual and ceremony, but every moment of their lives is suffused with playfulness, humour and a wonderful sense of fun. When we can consciously call on this vivid sense of joy and celebration—which they will give to us free-heartedly once we have made the effort to draw close to them—we will begin to learn that our own prayer, ritual and ceremony for communion with the spiritual world can be a constant theme of our days, offered continually at a deep inner level yet always spontaneous, natural and joyful.

7

Fairy Healing

---- ✳ ----

Considering the deep association that the fairies have with the moon, the world of nature, the angels and the Great Goddess, it would seem to be a matter of course that the spiritual feminine principle and the Good Folk must be closely linked. This indeed appears to be so: human women and the fairies share a special soul-relationship, although, since the spiritual feminine dwells within every heart, men certainly need not feel left out of the equation.

The beautiful old Gaelic tale of the Fairy Queen, recounted as history, casts light on this soul-relationship. The story, called 'The Fairy Queen and the Cup of Mary'—Ma, and other variations of the name Mary, have been given throughout history to the Mother Goddess, or to earthly representations of her—sets the Fairy Queen within the Tree of Life, that ancient living symbol of spirit dwelling on earth, with its roots nourished in the dark secret depths and its crown spanning the heavens:

> The maiden-queen of wisdom dwelt
> In the Beautiful Bower of the One Tree,
> Where she could see the world entire,
> And where no fool could look on her.

The Fairy Queen was deeply grieved 'at seeing the want of wisdom in the daughters of men'. She magically imbued every

herb and tree throughout the world with an occult message to all women, so that every growing thing breathed forth her invitation to come to the fairy knoll, so that she herself could give them wisdom.

The story tells how many women came in answer to the Fairy Queen's invitation, and how many did not. When they were all gathered together she appeared with the Cup of Mary, the blue-eyed limpet shell containing the 'wisdom of wisdoms', in her hands. This she held aloft, and all the women were invited to come and drink from it. So it was that 'to all who sought wisdom in their hearts the Fairy Queen gave of the Wisdom—to each according to her faith and desire'. Some women came too late to drink from the Cup of Mary, and others refused it—which is why, the tale ends, 'some women are wise and some are not'. Yet 'woman' means 'the spirit of wisdom', and if all who seek woman's mysteries will listen in silence to the voice of the heart (not the emotions), then all can receive from this Cup of Mary, or sacred well within the heart.

Fairies certainly have the power to heal, and in all countries a knowledge of the virtues of herbs can be traced back in mythology to the teachings of fairy women and of angels, who, as we have seen, are closely connected with the fairies. The fairies will often give us in our dreams the name of a particular herb needed to cure illness, so when you need such advice it is worth asking them to do so, with due courtesy, before settling down to sleep. Leave a notepad and pen handy, as you will be woken for a few moments so that you can memorise their recommendation. Of course, always check that any herb that may be suggested is safe for human consumption!

Wash your feet, your forehead and your hands as ritual purification before setting out on any herb-gathering mission. When gathering healing herbs, ask the fairies to guide you to those which contain the greatest life-force. Pass the first plant by, then take only what you need. Bless the herb, and speak to it as you take it, thanking it for giving of itself to make you whole. Gather always in a waxing moon—and all the better if it can be done on one of the fairy days. Try to do your herb-gathering in Raphael's, Anael's, Michael's or Gabriel's hour (see page 8). In this way, you will be sure to procure the goodwill and blessings of the fairies, who will add their power to your acts of healing and to the vitality of the herb itself.

Of course, the fairies can cure simply by magic, and where magic is concerned, a ritual is needed. The fairy spell that follows is a simple, natural ceremony which attracts and conducts their magic.

A Fairy Healing Spell

THE SACRED HEARTH AND HEATHER SPELL FOR THE CURE

OF ALL SKIN AILMENTS

> Procure a little hand-besom of heather (better still if you make it yourself) and get up in the morning at sunrise. Eat nothing and say nothing, but go straight to the hearth and brush all the ashes and cinders into a corner so that it is swept clean. Then bend over and spit upon the newly swept hearth, put the index finger of the right hand into the spittle and with it make the sign of the cross on the affected area of the skin, letting your touch be light but firm. Work this spell in the same way on nine successive mornings, and your skin troubles will disappear.

Even where an open fire is no longer used, many living-rooms still have a hearth; the spell is even said to work if a few pine-cones are burnt in a pot, and their ashes scattered on the hearth before going to bed.

8

Seeing and Talking with the Fairies

---- ✳ ----

We have to encounter and overcome many different 'skins' of ether before we can see the fairies and join them in brotherhood once more; these skins are the veil that humanity has woven to insulate itself from the fairies and the angels and the immediacy of the invisible spiritual worlds. When you have achieved this breakthrough in fairy vision, you will hear what the fairies have to say to you in the same way that you hear everything else; but until you have reached this level of development, hearing what the fairies say is a matter of listening with the heart.

The best way to do this is to empty ourselves of all our human woes and worries, as well as of the general clamour that goes on at the mental level. Embrace the silence; withdraw into the silence. Breathe the heavenly light of the six-pointed star which heals and makes all things new. In this soothing silence, lay down your earthly burdens and become a child again—an idealised child, we might say, since our human childhood is not without its stresses and problems. Yet we must all, at some carefree and happy moment when we were young, have expressed the ideal childhood spirit. It is this spirit of innocence that we need to rediscover.

In this state, perform one of the fairy spells. Then, asking your intuition to guide you, set out on a country walk, preferably somewhere off the beaten track where you can leave the road and enter a meadow or wood. Talking and listening to the fairies can even be done at home in the form of a meditation, as long as, before beginning to meditate, you contemplate the serenity and loveliness of nature so as to draw close to her. It is good to have a house-plant or some cut flowers from the garden in front of you so that you can make heart contact with the nature spirits; reading nature poetry, listening to beautiful music—not popular or light music because this inhibits, and in some cases throttles, the life forces—and studying tranquil art all further this process. Fairies are telepathic, and once you have contacted them and call on them matter and space are of no real consequence to them. But it is better, initially, to seek direct contact out in the wilds.

In order for the fairies to speak to you, you must first speak to *them*. It is very important to understand that you must always initiate contact. The fairies are shy, and timid of our coarser, material reality. They are curious about, and in a certain way even fascinated by, humans; but they are mindful of us, too, as destroyers and polluters—polluters not only of the natural environment but also of the ethers. We have to remember that we have caused terrible and ugly pollution of the most distressing proportions at the etheric level. And yet the ethers should be so beautiful, because etheric matter is refined and pliable and can create greater and purer beauty than any that can fully manifest on Earth, even though the two planes interconnect.

Because of the ethers' pliability, the dreadful pollution we have caused can be cleared much more simply than our pollution of the Earth. We can purify the ethers by good thought, kindly thought, thought that is loving, sensitive and artistic. If we emanate such thoughts as we seek out the fairies, they will recognise us and our intent as if we were giving out a password, or a secret code. It will pacify them a little for all human wrongdoing, past and present, and reassure them that we are not despoilers; although, of course there should always be absolute sincerity in our purpose— the fairies cannot be fooled. The fairies do not intellectualise, but they see truth, and they have access to vast reservoirs of intelligence and wisdom. So we must respect their doubts and uncertainties about us and do all we can to help them, with our thoughts and

spiritual attunement in creating lovely forms in the ethers which will begin to clear the pollution there, and by our actions in our outer life as we live on and respond to the Earth.

Send forth such loving, kindly thoughts to the fairies as you walk; and speak to them naturally and unselfconsciously in your heart, or even aloud if you are very sure there is no one else about! Thank them for their tireless work in the nature kingdom; let them know how deeply you appreciate the forms and colours of the trees and flowers, the herbs and the grass. And then, when you have found a spot to rest, begin to gaze deeply into the heart of nature. Step inside the outer form of the plants and trees around you, and see the spiritual life behind their material substance rising as pure white light within the sap which brings them sustenance from Mother Earth. Look deep into the lovely forms of the flowers and the trees and you will see the essence of their spirit dance and play as a rarefied white flame within their bodily structure. This is the love and laughter of the Goddess as she smiles upon the Earth, charging her fairies and angels to vivify and create all nature anew. The blessed white flame of the Goddess that burns in the shrine of her heart is courted by every visible form in the natural world. Each living sculpture, every shade of colour, has a story to tell of the inner worlds; and when you see with your inner eye the rising of the white light within each plant and tree, the fairies will approach very close to you.

Continue to tell them of your love for the Earth and your appreciation of their work, and then listen closely with your heart-mind. It is not a case of listening *hard*, but rather of listening tenderly, with all your being ... and the response will come. Sometimes the fairies use symbols rather than words, and they will take you into their worlds for a moment and give you a spiritual lesson or experience. At other times they will use words, or communicated intelligence, which will rise like a bubbling fountain in your mind so that you know what they are saying.

Where the fairies are concerned, hearing really comes before seeing, because you will need to speak to them in your heart, perhaps several times as you sit in solitude and silence, revisiting

your chosen spot, before they will venture to trust you; and when they begin to communicate with you, it is likely that some time will elapse before they allow you to see their ethereal forms shimmering in the sunlight, or appearing like the lineaments of a dream as they dance translucent through soft mists and gentle rain.

To see the fairies, do not turn your full gaze upon them, or they will disappear! Look at them only from the corner of the eye, keeping your study of them unchallenging and unconfrontational. Remember that it is a privilege that they appear to you. Send a gentle and tender outpouring of that spiritual white light from the heart of the six-pointed star, which is directly connected to your own heart, and you will bless the fairies and the work that they do. They will feel this blessing, and, in time, will return it.

This kind of giving and receiving can be done at the outer level too, with little offerings on your part. Traditionally, they appreciate a pat of good butter, a little jar of home-made preserve, a bowl of punch or wine, a cupful of milk or honey, or a little cake that you have baked for them, using the finest ingredients. Always ensure that any gift you offer the fairies is of the very best, and of natural and organic constitution. Say firmly, 'This is for the fairies', and leave it on a grassy knoll, beneath a bush or fairy tree. Give it with love and blessings, and the fairies will reward you with a host of sweet and simple miracles which will shower into your everyday life like fairy gold.

When visiting Turkey a few years ago I found myself on a wild stretch of moorland beside the Aegean Sea, and as it was quite deserted I decided to make a gift to the fairies of a lilting Irish reel that I had learned in my childhood—gifts of verse, song, music and dance are even more deeply appreciated by the fairies than material gifts. I thought that the Turkish fairies would like the Celtic flavour of the tune! Having performed my reel at sundown, when setting out for another walk the next morning I immediately came across a cowbell glimmering in the sun on the road. I had noted with special delight the tinkling bells on the collars of the elegant Turkish cows as they crossed the moor; and nothing could ever persuade me that nimble fairy fingers had not loosened that particular bell to make it fall where I could find it, in appreciation of my musical gift of the night before!

Such charming little incidents take place all the time when one begins to communicate with and make gifts to the fairies. And perhaps their greatest gift to us in the future—and, to anyone who seeks them with a sincere heart, in the present—will be to teach us to know once more the art of fun-filled living without the aid of drugs, alcohol or other mood-inducing stimulants, which draw from the lower, lurid astral planes. There are levels of life so much more intensely beautiful, rewarding and fulfilling than these grotesque astral pits that produce violence and suffering, if only we could remember how to gain access to them.

Drugs have always been used, in strict conformity with cosmic laws, to open up and charge the chakras so that the eyes of the spirit might open too. But it is interesting to note that the wholesale, undisciplined and ignorant use of these highly dangerous substances—dangerous from a spiritual viewpoint even more than from a physical one—started in earnest at the point when our vision finally closed on the fairy worlds, as the Industrial Revolution began to intensify. It was thus that we came to lose our perception of the nature spirits and of the 'cloths of heaven' that their enchanted worlds spread before us, reminding us that we are spiritual in essence and creatures of eternity.

The loss we continually feel at the soul level expresses itself as destructiveness in society. The fairies will teach us to take the first steps 'back home', by obviating the need for those unwise stimulants that exist in order to degrade and enslave humanity. When we learn from the fairies to feed our souls on a sense of liberation, exhilaration and the enjoyment that arises from simple and natural pleasures, the path that leads to these higher realms will begin to clear before us.

Before humanity's deep, deep descent into matter—a decline that culminated at the point when atomic bombs were discharged over Hiroshima and Nagasaki—there was a golden age. It was a time long, long ago, when humankind and the fairies could see and talk to one another freely, when there was love, understanding

and co-operation between their worlds, when men and women walked with angels, and Earth was a paradise. Life lived, and food grown, in co-operation with angelic beings and with the fairies, brought perfect physical and spiritual health to humankind. No war was perpetrated, no animals were slain; life was an ever-unfolding, passionately beautiful cosmic adventure; so much so that it was decided that humanity should embrace the challenge of a journey into the most profound fastnesses of unredeemed matter . . . and thus it was that human beings set out on the path to the heart of darkness, and loss upon loss ensued. But now it is time to struggle free from the grip of Ahriman, Lord of Darkness, and his consort the False Light—and turn back at last to our true home.

As we begin once again to welcome the fairies back into our lives, both the noble fays and the laughing, dancing elves, as we open our hearts and minds more and more to the creative forces of the universe so that we can begin to see the wonders of nature's hidden spiritual life, so we shall see that her designs and her beauties are the ideation of our higher selves—the very essence of our true human 'nature', which is spirit—expressed in outward form. This kingdom of nature, ensouled by the fairies, gives our own souls the perfect environment for the ideal expression of art, harmony and beauty, which are the flowers of love-in-action.

Nature's challenges exist not to incline us towards the philosophy that callousness and ruthlessness are the real laws and dynamics of life—a philosophy which, as our economic climate shows, we have deeply ingested and with which we at present identify—but to teach us to reach into ourselves and call down the powers of a higher dispensation, the powers of the spirit. We have seriously misinterpreted the lessons that nature has offered us, because we cannot see or comprehend her joyous company of fairies and angels, or the divine love that they express. Yet, as we begin to awaken once again to her mysteries and truths, so that former ideal state of life will be born again in the heart of every member of humanity. And the fairies, our rediscovered friends, will bring a superabundance of joy as their gift to our newborn paradise.

PICTURE CREDITS